I0759857

A LITTLE BOOK
of SELF-CARE
for THE
COLLEGE-BOUND

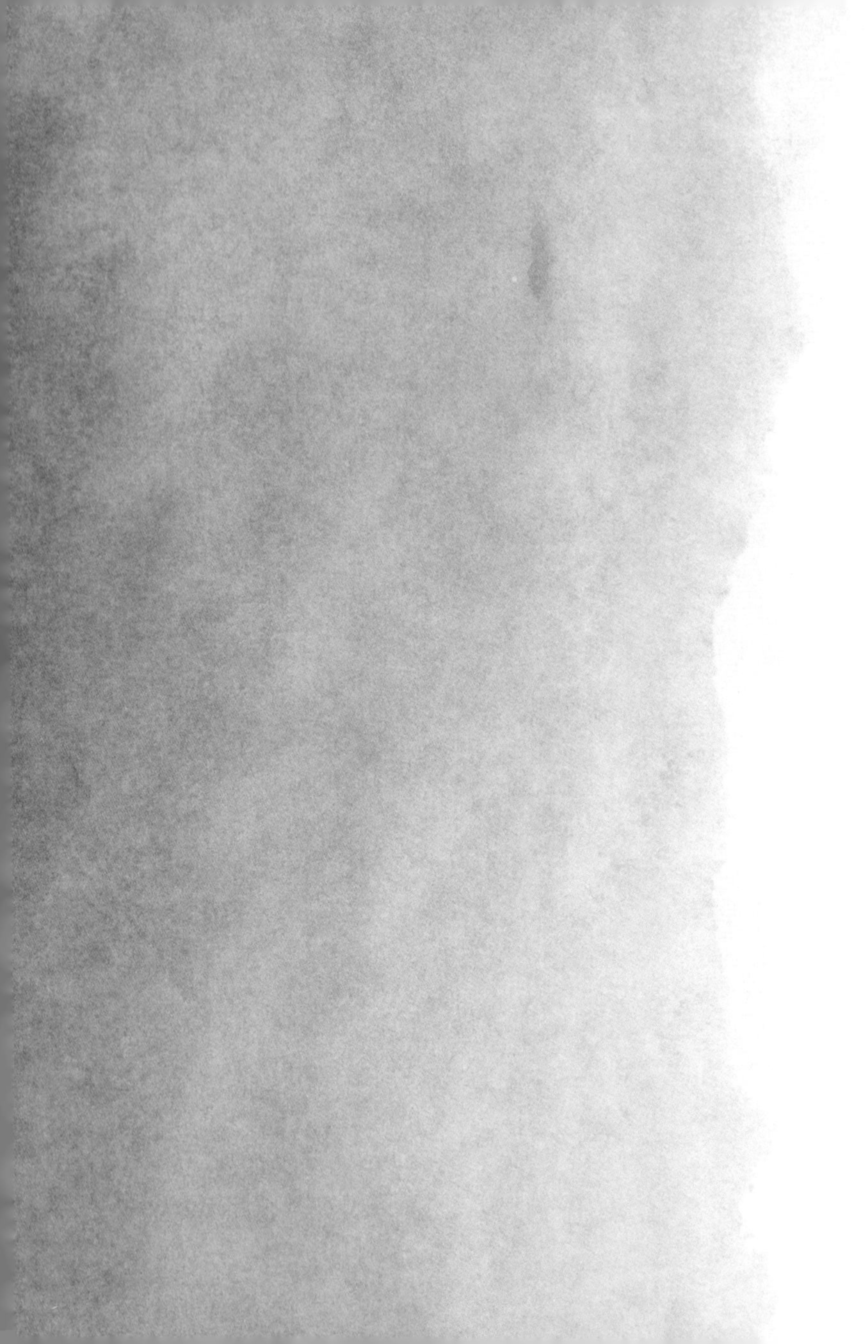

A LITTLE BOOK *of* SELF-CARE *for* THE COLLEGE-BOUND

with a foreword by
JENNIE MARIE BATTISTIN, MA, LMFT

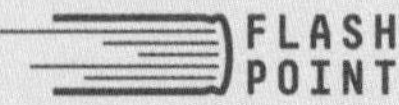

Published by Flashpoint™ Books, Seattle
www.flashpointbooks.com

Produced by Girl Friday Productions

Design: Rachel Marek
Development & editorial: Emilie Sandoz-Voyer
Production editorial: Katherine Richards

Image credits (all credits belong to Shutterstock users): cover (books), 33, lemoonkate; cover (watercolor), ii, x, 80, white snow; vi, SvetaArtStore; 3, Olga_C; 7, 61, 110, lavendertime; 9, Charlotte Ulrich; 12, Tiana Geo; 15, A_Berillo; 17, 109, Artnizu; 18, OrangeBySvetlana; 21, Atomorfen Illustration; 25, My Ho; 26, darina.ill; 29, 46, 103, 122, 124, Ayan Saqib; 34, Ekaterina Koniukhova; 37, 82, mimomy; 10–11, 38, 49, 125, xnova; 40 (popcorn), Daria Ustiugova; 40 (remote), 75, Maltiase; 43, 97, Mis vector; 44, 113, ArtCreationsDesignPhoto; 47, 72, 73, 88, 89, 115, Unchalee Khun; 51, Finkha; 57, Silmairel; 62, St_range Elena Platova; 65, 87, Cat_arch_angel; 66, Arsenova Natali; 70, 79, mimibubu; 76, Valentina Sova; 92, iri.art; 100, Alisles; 105, Julia August; 118, Vera Spasskaia; 121, Elizaveta Ruzanova; 127, Ekaterina Mikheeva; 132, Ermakova Marina

ISBN (hardcover): 978-1-964721-19-4
ISBN (ebook): 978-1-964721-20-0

Library of Congress Control Number: 2024919942

Printed in China

First edition

The information provided in this book is for educational purposes only. It is not a substitute for professional medical advice. If you are experiencing potential physical issues or having thoughts of self-harm, reach out to a trusted individual so they can help you find appropriate care.

FOREWORD

For many, college feels like the first step on the path to adulthood. College equals independence, freedom, and opportunity. It's where you'll make friends you might have for the rest of your life. It's where you'll find your passion, the one that will lead you to the career of your dreams. It's where new experiences present themselves every day—and all you have to do is reach out and grab them.

Sounds fun, right? But maybe it also sounds like a lot of pressure. Because that's the flip side of all the excitement college brings—many young people don't just feel the pressure to do well in school but also to enjoy every minute of it. And when those stressors overlap, the anxiety feedback loop becomes hard to control. Having worked with many young adults during their transition to college and throughout their college years, I've seen how easily they can become tangled in stress.

Here's the good news: you can take control and find balance through self-care. Just like brushing your teeth, self-care ideally needs to be a regular habit. It can be as simple as an easy breathing exercise, a guided meditation, or a quick activity to pull you out of a rut. Once you start thinking about it regularly, it can become a part of your life every day. Consistent self-care practice can transform how you approach and experience your college journey.

A Little Book of Self-Care for the College-Bound offers gentle advice and uplifting words to help you start and maintain your self-care practice. This book is here to support you in navigating the ups and downs of higher education while keeping your mental health at the forefront. Believe in yourself—you've got this!

—Jennie Marie Battistin, MA, LMFT,
author of *The Mindfulness Journal for Teens* and
Mindfulness for Teens in 10 Minutes a Day

“Learning is not attained by chance; it must be sought after with ardor and attended to with diligence.”

—Abigail Adams

INTRODUCTION

Getting here wasn't easy. In fact, it was a roller coaster, and it was exhausting. You started by applying to colleges—thinking about where you wanted to go, writing essays, gathering information, and then waiting for the decisions to roll in. When they finally arrived, and you figured out where you'd be going next, you went from being stressed out to feeling totally elated, celebrating your future with the people who love you. With the whirlwind of graduation and the excitement of packing, there isn't much time to sit and reflect on what comes next.

Most adults will tell you that college was the best time of their lives. They will reminisce about their carefree years and might forget to mention the moments of stress and sadness that accompanied the joy and fun. If you ask them to dig into their memories and be honest with themselves, every single one of those "wish I could do it again" adults in your life will tell you that there were times when things were hard. When you're in college, you're an adult, charting your own course. You're in a new place with new people, getting ready for new classes, with a whole campus to navigate. It can be a little overwhelming.

That's what this book is for. With advice from current and former college students, consider this a friendly resource anytime you're feeling sad, tired, frustrated, or in need of a little pick-me-up. Your classes are important, but your mental, physical, and emotional health are paramount. Whether you read this book all at once, flip through it at random, or try something new every day, it's designed to help you take care of *you*. Because the most important thing you can do in college is grow into your future self—and feel strong and supported doing it.

"And now that you don't have
to be perfect, you can be good."

—John Steinbeck

Breathe. Just breathe.

It's the best way to calm
frazzled nerves.

If you're feeling homesick, look up at the sky. It's the same one that your friends and family back home see, too. You are always connected to them.

"You must live in the
present, launch yourself
on every wave, find your
eternity in each moment."

—Henry David Thoreau

Take care of your body.
Eat real food. Rest.
Drink water. Exercise.

Asking for help is a
sign of strength.

Your school has counseling
and mental health services
available, should you need them.
They are there to be used.

When things are feeling overwhelmingly stressful, close your laptop and take a ten-minute movement break—on campus, around the library, or even in the dorm halls.

Join a sport—most schools have low-key intramural options.

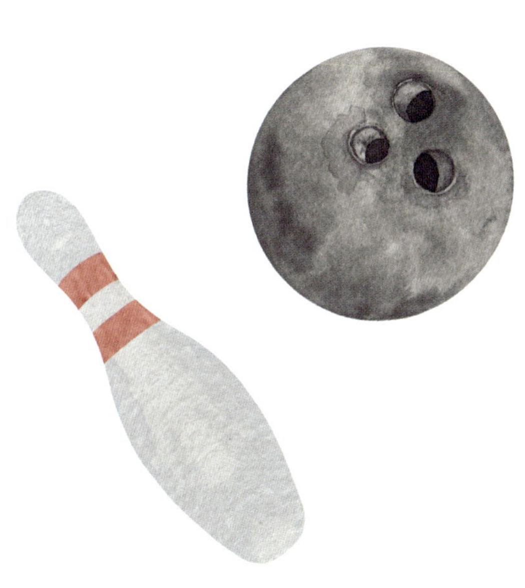

It's okay not to have
it all figured out.

“Courage is more
exhilarating than fear
and in the long run
it is easier.”

—Eleanor Roosevelt

Start your morning with
a full glass of water.

A warm shower is the ultimate hard reset. Things usually look a little better when you are clean and refreshed.

Every seemingly insurmountable problem gets easier when you break it into small steps.

Make a to-do list of all
the micro-level things that
need to get done in order
to accomplish the big thing
standing in your way. Then
start on just *one* step for now.

If you're feeling down, *dance.*
Lock your door, put on your
headphones, turn up your
favorite song, and dance like
no one's watching (because
no one's watching).

You don't have to be best friends with your roommate (if you have one). But try to establish some ground rules for respect and communication so bad feelings don't have space to fester.

Go chat with a professor. The real ones actually like their students and give great advice. It will also make you memorable and may even boost your grade.

“Nothing in life is to be feared;
it is only to be understood.”

—Marie Curie

Everyone is doing this
for the first time.

Don't be fooled by people
who seem like they have
it all figured out.

Help someone with their homework. Being helpful is a great mood booster.

1 2 3 4 5 6
7 8 9 10 11 12 13
14 15 16 17 18 19 20
21 22 23 24 25 26 27
28 29 30

Set up a weekly call
with someone from
home that you miss.

Buy some cookie or brownie mix and bake them up in the dorm kitchen. You're sure to make new friends that way.

"If you don't like something, change it. If you can't change it, change your attitude."

—Maya Angelou

Saying yes to life is great, but it's also okay to say no sometimes. You can say no to the party when you are already exhausted and running on empty, no to the activity that you just don't have the time for, no to the extra shift at work. Give yourself the space you need to create moments of calm.

Take a Saturday afternoon
off to binge a few episodes
of your favorite show.

Eat your vegetables.

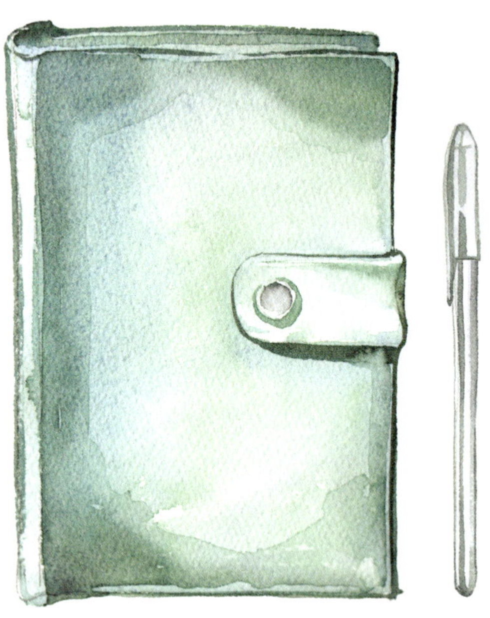

Start a journal. Write in it at least once a week and give yourself permission to be honest.

"Ignite the mind's spark
to rise the sun in you."

—Florence Nightingale

Go out to a show—music, improv, drama, or whatever is happening on campus this week. Try something new.

Your value is so much
more than your grades.

"I'm good enough, I'm smart enough, and doggone it, people like me."

—Al Franken, as Stuart Smalley

Make a list of every coffee shop on campus and try your favorite drink at each one. Which one is the hands-down best?

Sleep.

Try box breathing—close your eyes and take a deep breath in through your nose for four seconds, hold it for four seconds, and then let the breath out slowly through your mouth for four seconds.

Repeat ten times and
feel your body relax.

Pay a compliment to someone you don't know very well. Maybe they made an excellent point in class, or they have amazing taste in shoes. Making someone else feel appreciated and seen will help you feel good, too.

You have permission to feel sorry for yourself when things are hard. But give yourself a time cap—say one hour.

Listen to sad songs and wallow in the unfairness of it all. Then take a shower, drink a glass of water, and go find a distraction.

Failure is crucial to learning.
Nobody is perfect.

"I have not failed. I've just found 10,000 ways that won't work."

—Thomas Edison

11
03

Take breaks. Every hour you study, give yourself fifteen minutes to stretch, listen to a few songs, or just move away from your work. Your body and brain will thank you.

Making new friends is difficult for everyone. Remember that people are far more alike than they are different, so find that commonality and focus on that. Do you both snowboard? Read vampire novels? Love tacos? Go enjoy that thing together.

Finals don't last forever. Make a fun plan for the day you finish your exams, so you have something to look forward to.

There are so many resources.
You don't have to figure
everything out on your own.

When you're stressed or confused, look for support. That might be going to your professor's office hours, checking out the writing center, forming a study group, or looking into free tutoring. You're not alone.

Stretch out your arms,
shoulders, and legs.
Unclench your body.

"You change the world
by being yourself."

—Yoko Ono

You have the power to
make healthy decisions.

Spend an hour on Sundays organizing your commitments for the week. Schedule out when you will get things done.

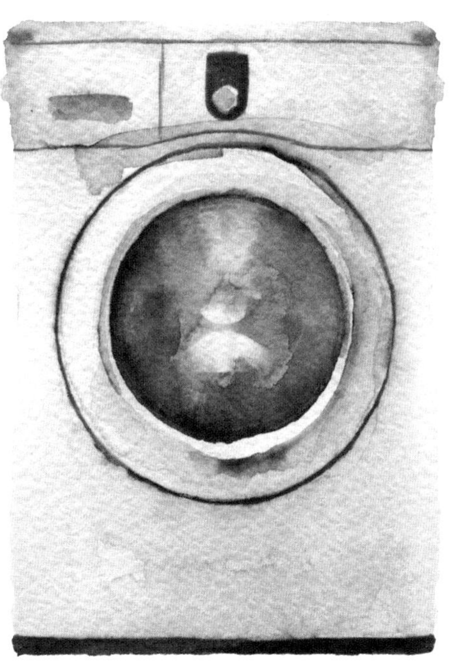

Find an evening routine and stick to it. Maybe it's a mug of tea, some calming music, and some light reading or journaling. Let your mind relax and power down before you try to sleep.

Find fun ways to move your body. Go for walks. Play Frisbee. Dance. Join a club. Do a workout video—or better yet, find an in-person workout class at the school gym.

"Beware; for I am fearless,
and therefore powerful."

—Mary Shelley

Be brave. It gets easier
every time.

Find a happy place to study
away from everyone else.
Maybe it has a great view. Or
great coffee. Or great music.

Know yourself. When
are you most productive
and motivated?

When are you *not*? Plan your study time accordingly.

Sketch, draw, or doodle.
Move a pen over paper.

"We need never be

ashamed of our tears."

—Charles Dickens

Call home when you need it.
Everyone feels homesick.

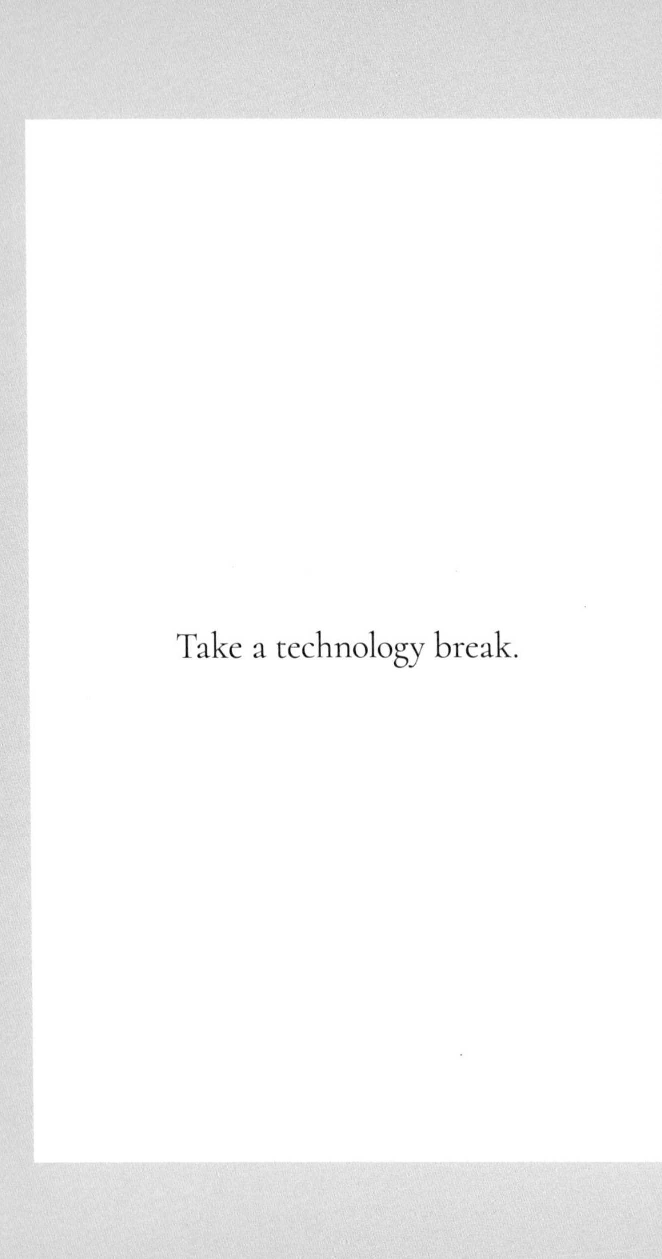

Take a technology break.

Put your phone face down
on your bed and leave it
there. Check on a friend,
read a book, grab a bite to
eat . . . but do it phone-free.

If you're heading to a party,
make sure hydration is
part of your game plan.

Lie down on your bed
and close your eyes. Focus
on relaxing each part of
your body in turn, from
your toes to your head.

Breathe deeply.

Close your eyes and visualize the most beautiful place you know. Try to experience it fully—imagine the sounds, recall the way it smells, and try to picture each feature of the landscape. Move through the space in your mind.

Make a plan for who you'll call
if you need help or support.

Friends, family members, professors, and advisors are all great places to start.

You belong here.

You are an adult now, but instead of focusing on the responsibilities that come with that, consider all the freedoms and opportunities you have now.

What can you do now that
you couldn't before?

Take a twenty-minute break to clean your working and living space. Start by simply decluttering your desk, making your bed, and putting away your clothes.

If you’re still deciding your major, connect with professors in the departments you’re considering majoring in to understand what kinds of classes you might be taking.

Do the classes sound
exciting and motivating?
That's a good sign.

You won't grow unless you make mistakes. Own them, face them, and move forward.

"There are many things
you can do overnight. . . .
But there is no such thing
as an overnight success."

—Tory Burch

"I'm not afraid of
storms, for I'm learning
how to sail my ship."

—Louisa May Alcott

When you're overwhelmed, make a list and give every task a time slot. Then tackle one thing at a time.

Before the semester or quarter starts, take a moment to find where all your classes are. Plan your route so you don't feel lost on your first day of class. And time your commute if you're living off campus.

Find somewhere to volunteer on or off campus, even if it's only once a month. Giving back to your community is a great way to feel connected to it.

"Do the best you can in
every task, no matter
how unimportant it may
seem at the time."

—Sandra Day O'Connor

Spend time off campus and see the sights in your college town.

Visit a well-known local restaurant, take the bus to a new coffee shop to study, or explore a local park.

Find a houseplant to take care of. Succulents require very little water. Enjoy its greenery, ease of care, and calming presence.

Connect with your RA if you're living in the residence halls. Despite what you hear, they're not just there to "bust" you. They are a great resource and can help you navigate your first year of college.

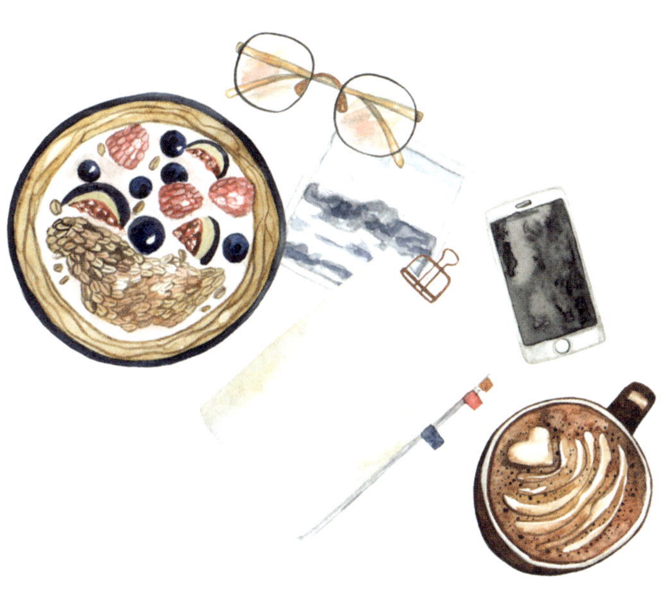

"An education isn't how much you have committed to memory, or even how much you know. It's being able to differentiate between what you know and what you don't."

—Anatole France

Set up a meeting with your academic advisor. They are there to keep you on track for graduation and make sure you're taking all the right classes.

"It's good to do uncomfortable things. It's weight training for life."

—Anne Lamott

Take a moment to appreciate how far you've come. Think through everything you've done to get to this point. Consider all the hard things you've worked through and the successes you've had.

Now look to the future. What challenges will you set for yourself next? What moments of joy will you seek out?

What will your bright
tomorrow look like?

RESOURCES

WEBSITES

The Mental Health Coalition
https://www.thementalhealthcoalition.org/college-mental-health-toolkit/

The American College Health Association
https://www.acha.org/ACHA/Resources/Topics/MentalHealth.aspx

Active Minds
https://www.activeminds.org/

Mental Health First Aid
https://www.mentalhealthfirstaid.org/

APPS

Headspace
www.headspace.com

Calm
www.calm.com

PODCASTS

The College Info Geek

For You from Eve

Life Kit

Tiny Leaps, Big Changes

The Psychology of Your 20s

Moments

BOOKS

Self-Care for College Students, by Julia Dellitt

175+ Things to Do Before You Graduate College, by Charlotte Lake

The Ultimate College Student Health Handbook, by Jill Grimes

The No-Worries Workbook, by Molly Burford

The Mindfulness Journal for Teens, by Jennie Marie Battistin

Mindfulness for Teens in 10 Minutes a Day, by Jennie Marie Battistin

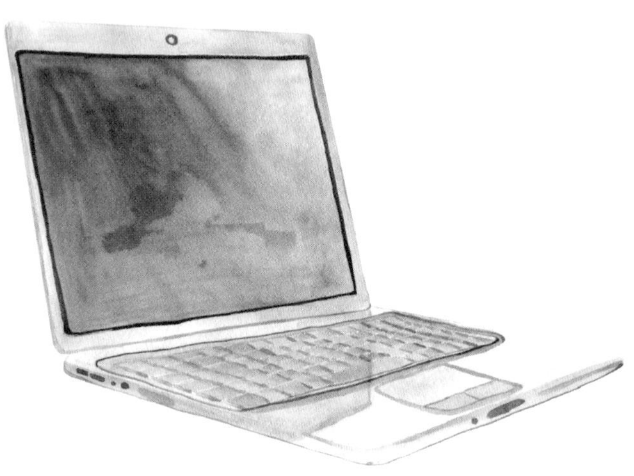

ABOUT THE FOREWORD AUTHOR

JENNIE MARIE BATTISTIN, MA, LMFT, graduated cum laude with a master's in clinical psychology from Pepperdine University. She has been a facilitator for *Angst: A Documentary on Anxiety*, which helped create a dialogue between parents and teens. Along with writing two bestselling books on teen mental health, Battistin is the founding director of Hope Therapy Center, Marriage and Family Counseling Inc. in California.

The gift of self-care is important in all life stages—check out all the titles in the A Little Book of Self-Care series:

A Little Book of Self-Care for Those Who Grieve

A Little Book of Self-Care for the College-Bound

A Little Book of Self-Care for Brides